Kakalimutan na lang kita
Wala rin naman akong magagawa
Kapag pinag patuloy ko pa ito
Magmumukha lang akong tanga

Depression calls out
It’s so dark in here alone
I might die later

Life's melancholy
Was difficult to remove
Until Death arrived

Sunrise and sunset
Not destined to ever meet
Just like you and me

First love never dies
I used to believe in that
Until I met you

No one can contest
You are my only dearest
At your worst or best

Was an atheist
'Til I saw she's a goddess
Now, my faith is hers

Sari-sari store
Ang Shopee at Lazada
Zalora damit

Locked my fragile heart
And isolated myself
My emotions, gone

Friendships come and go
No forever promises
So glad I met you

By their pure talents,
Artists can make immortals
From any models

Artists and writers
Making worlds out of nowhere
T**echnically gods**

I’m the devil from your dreams
Yet you choose to keep me
Because you know how I feel
And I’m the only one that’s real

This is a haiku
About **moving on from you**
No other words yet

Soft curly long hair
Kissable lips, tender eyes
I'll retract her name (CD)

Morning iced coffee
Eggs, bacons, and garlic rice
Perfect way to start

North pole to south pole
If it's a matter of love
It's walking distance

Why complicate things
You love me and I love you
Let's make it simple

Midnight snack drive thru
Just you and me strolling
Perfect date indeed

Expensive coffee
But if together with you
Totally worth it

Blooming sunflowers
Equals happy sad goodbyes
Opening new world

3 in the morning
Can't sleep at all, fearing that
You'll be in my dreams

Too political?!?
Silence helps the oppressor
It's not neutral stance

Innocent lives gone
This world is ending right now
Conflicts must be stop

Aphrodite's Conclusion

Stunned by the beauty of Aphrodite
She smiled at me like Mona Lisa did
It is pretty yet full of mystery
How to respond to a face I can't read
I feared that her expression is just fake
But it is my anxiety talking
I trust my instincts she's not a snake
For this is a pure-goddess I'm seeing
Already confessed my feelings for her
Way before I saw this wonderful view
Gave her a letter and a sunflower
For her it is something out of the blue
Appreciated and I'm still her friend
For it is the greatest love she can send

Sonnet for my country

Here he comes, the infamous Mister Lee
With his grumpy face, he walks to get Juan
Everyday it's his hobby to bully
Mainly to Juan who doesn't know how to run
Juan has the support of his many friends
Yet he refuses to fight for the right
For his dad claims he's not worth to defend
Juan loses confidence from his one light
In fact, his dad thinks something different
Lee is his inspiration, a savior
Deafen, hearing Lee is magnificent
Blinded, seeing only good behavior
One cry stands out for Juan though, his mother
Only thing that keeps him warm and better.

A Colored Country

White, blue, green, what's your favorite color?
My country has two, it's red or yellow
Three, since brown's included said a joker
I never felt my country very low
It's a false dichotomy they allow
Most believed that they're a righteous person
They'll do anything to make us bow
Virtue of their color is a lesson
Blinded by each other's truth, we're at war
And innocents suffer in this conflict
Colors involve should be held accounted for
As our country gained pain not benefit
Peace may be impossible instantly
So, talking should be a priority

No Freedom In Here

No one has the right to be on standby
In this country no man is innocent
EVERYONE can be arrested or die
Since it's right and just said the government
Its leader doesn't understand his powers
For he thinks everything is just a jest
And he thinks his mouth contains all answers
He gives orders for his self interest
We, the citizens are no longer free
We may have our rights, but we LIVE IN FEAR
A fear that we'll be in his killing spree
Here EVERYONE IS IN THE GUILTY TIER
We should not tolerate this kind of act
For every citizen should feel intact

Invalid Logic

A friend asked me why I did not court her
I said "she's the most wonderful person
And she doesn't deserve some kind of monster"
Honestly it is not just the reason
I'm contented and happy as her friend
For it's this way where no one could get pain
And it is a bond that is hard to end
Since I'm afraid to have more loss than gain
Next reason is my own anxiety
This one I received a lot from the past
Fear, it'll create illogicality
Not to mention, this basis isn't my last
Part of me wants to court her really
But I am full of reasons as you can see

Through Effort and Cheating

I tried so hard to conceal my feelings
Yet here I am thinking how to confess
Fondness for her I'll put in my writings
I'll make the EFFORT for she’s a goddess
I wrote everything I wanted to say
A very old-style love letter I did
Took more time than writing a school essay
It was handwritten with terrible speed
Wondering if this is not enough yet
I've got to give her something more than this
A sunflower and sincere gift should set
This hopeless romantic's current crisis
Terrified, I asked her about my plan
She said it's nice thinking it's for someone

And It All Begins

Daily routine ruined by this lady
Consistently, I eat, study, and play
Never thought I would fall for somebody
For I'm occupied every single day
I always thought I'm fine the way I am
Until the moment that I noticed her
I began to doubt my daily system
I saw in her that I can do better
She pulled me out of my deep comfort zone
I now do things I've never done before
And my life is no longer monotone
Thanks to this lady I truly adore
She broke my usual incompetence
For she's one of my greatest influence

Alien's Charismatic Mentor

You made feel that I belong in here
In this large, unknown world where I'm adrift
Guided me for you're an overseer
Taught me how in this place I can make shift
Years I've been here and was an alien
No friends and afraid to talk to people
Then you came, with chance's doors you open
Connecting with others, you made simple
When you said we got here at the same day
I admired that you've achieved many things
By characteristics that you display
Thank you for passing them through your teachings
You said goodbye when the sunflowers grown
Leaving the lesson to stand on my own

Yet They Blame Me

I always ask myself why they can't see
That I'm the victim and not the sinner.
Are they really that blind to blame me?
These accusations make me more suffer.
They thought I wanted what happened. But NO!
They'd been judging types of the clothes I wear
Or pointing out that I act like a ho
Equal to the offender they declare
This culture needs to die for true justice
No wrong charges are made except for one
They who made me guilty with their premise
Fallacies they have repeatedly done
The deed was done alone by the culprit
Yet they blame me as if I asked for it

Christelle

I cannot find the perfect word to describe thee
For thy perfection can't be comprehended by me
For the thought of thee makes my heart beat faster
Thou, who when I see, makes me stutter.

Thy eyes contain secrets of the world
A mystery I always wanted to unfold
Thy curly hair that I love
Which color(s) next will it have?
Thy voice that I once heard long ago
I needed to hear it once more, I know
And our chats about things we have in common
I wish that we had a ton

I tried asking thy time
Once? Twice? it almost feels like a crime
My own progress stopped on that last no
I never wanted to go back to never ask thou
All I want now is to move forward again
Leaving behind all this pain

That's when I decided I needed to push thee away
For I don't know if this is obsession
I hope one day thou will forgive me
Because I do know I will not stop loving thee

Shan't

I shall not rest
Not when my government's a burden to its people
Not when the privileged doesn't sympathize the oppressed
Especially not when a tyrant thinks he's the best

I shall not concede
Not to someone who sells his own country and forsake it's people
Not to someone who can't admit his failures and eluded what's real
Especially not to a king whose policy is to kill

I shall not cower in fear
Not to those people who think injustice can be justified
Not to those people whose tongue is sharper than their own mind
Especially not to those people who would spread misinformation and turn blind

We shall not falter
Not until everyone are united against fascism
Not until everyone understands that activism is NOT terrorism
Especially not until everyone agrees this country deserves better

Queen's Homecoming

It has been seven years
When you dared to conquer the seven seas
Usually, when I think about it
It would bring me to tears

Endless summers have passed
Yet it felt winter
Longed for your warm love
From our old memories that linger

Then, I began to doubt
That you will ever come back
I stopped thinking about
The promise that you've probably forgotten

But when I heard in our town
Your ship was here
I rushed, only to find you
Resting under the sea you hold dear.

The Stupid King

Thou who barged into the castle
Glorious was thee to break such fragile thing
Even if fortified with sentinels
Thy appeal is no match for a king

Thou who knew how to defend
Thy self from any siege
King's reign came to an end
When thy forces into his kingdom you reach

That king is at fault
For his overconfidence took over
Thy own queendom he tried to assault
Yet ye proven again to be better

Now the king lost his confidence
For he never established a better defense

It Started With Schrödinger's cat

Gave thought about my feelings
And like what a sitcom said, Schrödinger's cat
We'll never know if it's a good thing
Unless we take a chance

Kept thinking, how to ask someone out
What better way than to craft an art
Even though I'm no master
Hoping this would open thy heart

No additional stanzas needed to persuade
Straight to the point I'll go, unafraid
So, I asked thee on one dinner date
Perhaps, before eight?

If it fails, I won't persist
We can still be friends at least.
But if we succeed,
Into the next level we can proceed

Moon and Stars

In this world where you're Artemis
How can I be your Orion?
For my feelings might easily dismissed
Unlike the goddess whose love
Turned a man into a constellation

As I gazed upon the moon
My heart beats faster
Wondered if it can hear it
Even though our distance grows larger

And as Helios rode his chariot
Tears ran down to my eyes
For again, I missed the opportunity
To say I love you
Before the goodbye

The Last?

I thought of writing but never knew how
Then I learned this very old art
And telling my stories it allowed
But I felt that there's still missing on my part

I knew how to express myself but never have exactly something about
Then I met her, Aphrodite, the one with Mona Lisa's smile
And suddenly got inspired, words in my head just got out
Although I thought that writing for her is out of style

I tried to keep writing even if the seasons shift.
The queen for fall, Aphrodite and technically a god for winter,
And the king slayer, and the queen again for summer
These pieces that I wrote, I tried giving them as a gift

I recognized that I'm no good but it never stopped me
What made me think of quitting is the queen
I fall for her twice, both failed and now I see
That no matter what I do, even in a million rhymes, my heart for her will never win.

I guess never again shall I write another poem
Until I find the only exception.

www.ingramcontent.com/pod-product-compliance
Ingram Content Group UK Ltd.
Pitfield, Milton Keynes, MK11 3LW, UK
UKHW041846200726
13854UKWH00005BA/2235

9 781458 317322